# 50 Mediterranean-Inspired Grilled Fish Recipes for Home

By: Kelly Johnson

# Table of Contents

- Grilled Lemon Garlic Mediterranean Sea Bass
- Greek-style Grilled Swordfish Skewers
- Italian Herb Marinated Grilled Halibut
- Moroccan Spiced Grilled Red Snapper
- Mediterranean Grilled Tuna Steaks
- Grilled Shrimp and Calamari Salad
- Lemon Oregano Grilled Mackerel
- Spanish Paprika Grilled Anchovies
- Herb-infused Grilled Branzino
- Tuscan Grilled Salmon with Balsamic Glaze
- Lebanese-style Grilled Cod with Sumac
- Herb Crusted Grilled Sardines
- Grilled Octopus with Mediterranean Marinade
- Sicilian-style Grilled Grouper
- Turkish Yogurt-marinated Grilled Trout
- Grilled Haddock with Tomato Caper Relish
- Lemon Basil Grilled Hake
- Greek Souvlaki-inspired Grilled Whitefish
- Mediterranean Stuffed Grilled Squid
- Grilled Tuna Nicoise Salad
- Moroccan Harissa Grilled Catfish
- Spanish Romesco Grilled Branzino
- Italian Lemon Rosemary Grilled Bass
- Greek Yogurt Marinated Grilled Mullet
- Grilled Swordfish with Mediterranean Salsa
- Tunisian Spiced Grilled Tilapia
- Herb-infused Grilled Red Mullet
- Grilled Shrimp with Olive Tapenade
- Lemon Za'atar Grilled Mackerel
- Mediterranean Grilled Gurnard with Fennel
- Spanish-style Grilled Herring
- Italian Balsamic Glazed Grilled Tuna
- Grilled Mediterranean Bluefish with Herbs
- Herb Crusted Grilled Cuttlefish
- Turkish Spiced Grilled Sea Bass
- Grilled Branzino with Lemon Caper Sauce
- Moroccan Charmoula Grilled Mackerel
- Greek Feta-stuffed Grilled Anchovies
- Sicilian-style Grilled Amberjack
- Lemon Garlic Grilled John Dory

- Italian Pesto Grilled Red Snapper
- Grilled Sardine Skewers with Lemon
- Spanish Romesco Grilled Mullet
- Mediterranean Grilled Mackinaw with Tomato
- Lebanese Sumac Grilled Porgy
- Greek-style Grilled Yellowtail
- Tuscan Herb Grilled Rainbow Trout
- Moroccan Ras el Hanout Grilled Perch
- Grilled Sea Bream with Mediterranean Vinaigrette
- Italian Herb Grilled Mahi-Mahi

**Grilled Lemon Garlic Mediterranean Sea Bass**

Ingredients:

- 4 fresh sea bass fillets
- 1/4 cup olive oil
- 3 cloves garlic, minced
- Zest of 1 lemon
- Juice of 1 lemon
- 1 teaspoon dried oregano
- 1 teaspoon dried thyme
- Salt and black pepper, to taste
- Lemon slices for garnish
- Fresh parsley, chopped, for garnish

Instructions:

Preheat your grill to medium-high heat.
In a small bowl, whisk together olive oil, minced garlic, lemon zest, lemon juice, dried oregano, dried thyme, salt, and black pepper to create the marinade.
Pat the sea bass fillets dry with paper towels and place them in a shallow dish or a resealable plastic bag.
Pour the marinade over the sea bass fillets, ensuring they are well-coated. Allow the fish to marinate for at least 30 minutes in the refrigerator, turning them occasionally to distribute the flavors evenly.
Remove the sea bass from the refrigerator and let it come to room temperature for about 10 minutes.
Grease the grill grates with a bit of oil to prevent sticking.
Place the sea bass fillets on the preheated grill, skin side down. Grill for about 4-5 minutes per side, or until the fish is opaque and easily flakes with a fork.
While grilling, baste the fillets with any remaining marinade to keep them moist and flavorful.
Once done, transfer the grilled sea bass to a serving platter.
Garnish with lemon slices and chopped fresh parsley.
Serve the Grilled Lemon Garlic Mediterranean Sea Bass hot, accompanied by your favorite Mediterranean sides like roasted vegetables, couscous, or a Greek salad. Enjoy!

**Greek-style Grilled Swordfish Skewers**

Ingredients:

- 1.5 lbs swordfish steaks, cut into 1-inch cubes
- 1/4 cup olive oil
- 3 tablespoons fresh lemon juice
- 2 cloves garlic, minced
- 1 teaspoon dried oregano
- 1 teaspoon dried thyme
- 1 teaspoon paprika
- Salt and black pepper, to taste
- Cherry tomatoes, for skewering
- Red onion, cut into chunks, for skewering
- Lemon wedges, for serving
- Fresh parsley, chopped, for garnish

Instructions:

In a bowl, whisk together olive oil, lemon juice, minced garlic, dried oregano, dried thyme, paprika, salt, and black pepper to create the marinade.
Cut the swordfish into 1-inch cubes and place them in a shallow dish. Pour the marinade over the swordfish, ensuring all pieces are well-coated. Marinate in the refrigerator for at least 30 minutes.
If you're using wooden skewers, soak them in water for about 30 minutes to prevent burning.
Preheat your grill to medium-high heat.
Thread the marinated swordfish cubes onto the skewers, alternating with cherry tomatoes and chunks of red onion.
Brush the skewers with a bit of olive oil to prevent sticking.
Place the swordfish skewers on the preheated grill and cook for about 3-4 minutes per side, or until the fish is cooked through and has a nice grill mark.
While grilling, you can baste the skewers with any remaining marinade for added flavor.
Once done, transfer the grilled swordfish skewers to a serving platter.
Garnish with fresh chopped parsley and serve with lemon wedges on the side.
Enjoy these Greek-style Grilled Swordfish Skewers with your favorite Mediterranean sides like Greek salad, tzatziki, or rice pilaf.

**Italian Herb Marinated Grilled Halibut**

Ingredients:

- 4 halibut fillets (6-8 ounces each)
- 1/4 cup olive oil
- 3 tablespoons fresh lemon juice
- 2 cloves garlic, minced
- 1 teaspoon dried oregano
- 1 teaspoon dried basil
- 1 teaspoon dried thyme
- Salt and black pepper, to taste
- Lemon wedges, for serving
- Fresh basil or parsley, chopped, for garnish

Instructions:

In a bowl, whisk together olive oil, fresh lemon juice, minced garlic, dried oregano, dried basil, dried thyme, salt, and black pepper to create the marinade.
Pat the halibut fillets dry with paper towels and place them in a shallow dish.
Pour the marinade over the fillets, ensuring they are well-coated. Marinate in the refrigerator for at least 30 minutes.
Preheat your grill to medium-high heat.
Remove the halibut fillets from the refrigerator and let them come to room temperature for about 10 minutes.
Grease the grill grates with a bit of oil to prevent sticking.
Place the halibut fillets on the preheated grill and cook for about 4-5 minutes per side, or until the fish is opaque and easily flakes with a fork.
While grilling, you can brush the fillets with any remaining marinade for added flavor.
Once done, transfer the grilled halibut to a serving platter.
Garnish with fresh chopped basil or parsley and serve with lemon wedges on the side.
Enjoy this Italian Herb Marinated Grilled Halibut with your favorite Italian-inspired sides like roasted vegetables, pasta, or a caprese salad.

**Moroccan Spiced Grilled Red Snapper**

Ingredients:

- 4 red snapper fillets
- 3 tablespoons olive oil
- 2 teaspoons ground cumin
- 1 teaspoon ground coriander
- 1 teaspoon smoked paprika
- 1 teaspoon ground cinnamon
- 1 teaspoon ground ginger
- 1 teaspoon ground turmeric
- 2 cloves garlic, minced
- Zest and juice of 1 lemon
- Salt and black pepper, to taste
- Fresh cilantro, chopped, for garnish
- Lemon wedges, for serving

Instructions:

In a bowl, combine olive oil, ground cumin, ground coriander, smoked paprika, ground cinnamon, ground ginger, ground turmeric, minced garlic, lemon zest, lemon juice, salt, and black pepper to create the spice marinade.

Pat the red snapper fillets dry with paper towels and place them in a shallow dish. Pour the spice marinade over the fillets, ensuring they are well-coated.

Marinate in the refrigerator for at least 30 minutes.

Preheat your grill to medium-high heat.

Remove the red snapper fillets from the refrigerator and let them come to room temperature for about 10 minutes.

Grease the grill grates with a bit of oil to prevent sticking.

Place the red snapper fillets on the preheated grill and cook for about 4-5 minutes per side, or until the fish is opaque and easily flakes with a fork.

While grilling, you can brush the fillets with any remaining spice marinade for added flavor.

Once done, transfer the grilled red snapper to a serving platter.

Garnish with fresh chopped cilantro and serve with lemon wedges on the side.

Enjoy this Moroccan Spiced Grilled Red Snapper with couscous, a side of harissa, or grilled vegetables for a complete Moroccan-inspired meal.

**Mediterranean Grilled Tuna Steaks**

Ingredients:

- 4 tuna steaks (6-8 ounces each)
- 1/4 cup olive oil
- 2 tablespoons balsamic vinegar
- 2 tablespoons soy sauce
- 3 cloves garlic, minced
- 1 teaspoon dried oregano
- 1 teaspoon dried thyme
- 1 teaspoon smoked paprika
- Salt and black pepper, to taste
- Lemon wedges, for serving
- Fresh parsley, chopped, for garnish

Instructions:

In a bowl, whisk together olive oil, balsamic vinegar, soy sauce, minced garlic, dried oregano, dried thyme, smoked paprika, salt, and black pepper to create the marinade.

Pat the tuna steaks dry with paper towels and place them in a shallow dish. Pour the marinade over the tuna steaks, ensuring they are well-coated. Marinate in the refrigerator for at least 30 minutes.

Preheat your grill to medium-high heat.

Remove the tuna steaks from the refrigerator and let them come to room temperature for about 10 minutes.

Grease the grill grates with a bit of oil to prevent sticking.

Place the tuna steaks on the preheated grill and cook for about 2-3 minutes per side for medium-rare, or longer if you prefer your tuna more well-done.

While grilling, you can brush the tuna steaks with any remaining marinade for added flavor.

Once done, transfer the grilled tuna steaks to a serving platter.

Garnish with fresh chopped parsley and serve with lemon wedges on the side.

Enjoy these Mediterranean Grilled Tuna Steaks with a side of quinoa, a simple salad, or grilled vegetables for a delightful Mediterranean-inspired meal.

**Grilled Shrimp and Calamari Salad**

Ingredients:

For the Grilled Shrimp and Calamari:

- 1 pound large shrimp, peeled and deveined
- 1 pound calamari, cleaned and tentacles separated
- 3 tablespoons olive oil
- 2 cloves garlic, minced
- 1 teaspoon smoked paprika
- Salt and black pepper, to taste
- Lemon wedges, for serving

For the Salad:

- Mixed salad greens (lettuce, arugula, spinach, etc.)
- Cherry tomatoes, halved
- Cucumber, sliced
- Red onion, thinly sliced
- Kalamata olives, pitted
- Feta cheese, crumbled
- Fresh parsley, chopped, for garnish

For the Dressing:

- 1/4 cup olive oil
- 2 tablespoons red wine vinegar
- 1 teaspoon Dijon mustard
- 1 teaspoon honey
- Salt and black pepper, to taste

Instructions:

In a bowl, combine olive oil, minced garlic, smoked paprika, salt, and black pepper. Toss the shrimp and calamari in the mixture until evenly coated. Marinate for about 15-30 minutes. Preheat your grill to medium-high heat.

Thread the shrimp and calamari tentacles onto skewers, or use a grilling basket to prevent small pieces from falling through the grates.

Grill the shrimp and calamari for 2-3 minutes per side or until they are cooked through and have a nice grill mark. Be careful not to overcook to keep them tender.

While grilling, prepare the salad by arranging mixed greens, cherry tomatoes, cucumber, red onion, Kalamata olives, and feta cheese on a serving platter or individual plates.

In a small bowl, whisk together olive oil, red wine vinegar, Dijon mustard, honey, salt, and black pepper to create the dressing.

Once the shrimp and calamari are grilled, remove them from the skewers or basket and arrange them on top of the salad.

Drizzle the dressing over the grilled shrimp and calamari salad.

Garnish with fresh chopped parsley and serve with lemon wedges on the side.

Enjoy this Grilled Shrimp and Calamari Salad as a refreshing and satisfying Mediterranean-inspired dish.

**Lemon Oregano Grilled Mackerel**

Ingredients:

- 4 mackerel fillets
- 1/4 cup olive oil
- 3 tablespoons fresh lemon juice
- 2 cloves garlic, minced
- 1 tablespoon fresh oregano, chopped (or 1 teaspoon dried oregano)
- Zest of 1 lemon
- Salt and black pepper, to taste
- Lemon wedges, for serving
- Fresh oregano, for garnish

Instructions:

In a bowl, whisk together olive oil, fresh lemon juice, minced garlic, chopped fresh oregano (or dried oregano), lemon zest, salt, and black pepper to create the marinade.

Pat the mackerel fillets dry with paper towels and place them in a shallow dish. Pour the marinade over the fillets, ensuring they are well-coated. Marinate in the refrigerator for at least 30 minutes.

Preheat your grill to medium-high heat.

Remove the mackerel fillets from the refrigerator and let them come to room temperature for about 10 minutes.

Grease the grill grates with a bit of oil to prevent sticking.

Place the mackerel fillets on the preheated grill and cook for about 3-4 minutes per side, or until the fish is opaque and easily flakes with a fork.

While grilling, you can brush the fillets with any remaining marinade for added flavor.

Once done, transfer the grilled mackerel to a serving platter.

Garnish with fresh oregano and serve with lemon wedges on the side.

Enjoy this Lemon Oregano Grilled Mackerel with a side of quinoa, a simple salad, or grilled vegetables for a delicious and light Mediterranean meal.

**Spanish Paprika Grilled Anchovies**

Ingredients:

- 1 pound fresh anchovies, cleaned and gutted
- 3 tablespoons olive oil
- 1 tablespoon smoked paprika (pimentón)
- 2 cloves garlic, minced
- 1 tablespoon fresh parsley, chopped
- Salt and black pepper, to taste
- Lemon wedges, for serving

Instructions:

Preheat your grill to medium-high heat.
In a small bowl, mix together olive oil, smoked paprika, minced garlic, chopped fresh parsley, salt, and black pepper to create the marinade.
Pat the anchovies dry with paper towels and place them in a shallow dish. Pour the marinade over the anchovies, ensuring they are well-coated. Marinate for about 15-30 minutes.
If you're using wooden skewers, soak them in water for about 30 minutes to prevent burning.
Thread the marinated anchovies onto skewers or place them directly on the grill grates.
Grill the anchovies for approximately 2-3 minutes per side or until they are cooked through and have a nice grill mark. Be careful not to overcook to keep them tender.
Once done, transfer the grilled anchovies to a serving platter.
Serve the Spanish Paprika Grilled Anchovies hot, garnished with additional chopped parsley, and accompanied by lemon wedges.
Enjoy this flavorful and aromatic dish as a tapas-style appetizer or part of a Spanish-inspired seafood feast.

**Herb-infused Grilled Branzino**

Ingredients:

- 2 whole branzino, gutted and scaled
- 1/4 cup olive oil
- 3 tablespoons fresh lemon juice
- 3 cloves garlic, minced
- 2 tablespoons fresh parsley, chopped
- 1 tablespoon fresh thyme leaves
- 1 tablespoon fresh rosemary, chopped
- Salt and black pepper, to taste
- Lemon slices, for stuffing
- Fresh herbs for garnish (parsley, thyme, rosemary)

Instructions:

Preheat your grill to medium-high heat.
In a bowl, whisk together olive oil, fresh lemon juice, minced garlic, chopped fresh parsley, fresh thyme leaves, fresh rosemary, salt, and black pepper to create the herb-infused marinade.
Pat the branzino dry with paper towels, inside and out. Make a few diagonal cuts on each side of the fish.
Rub the herb-infused marinade all over the branzino, making sure to get the marinade inside the cuts and cavity of the fish. Allow the fish to marinate for at least 30 minutes.
Stuff the cavity of each branzino with lemon slices.
Grease the grill grates with a bit of oil to prevent sticking.
Place the branzino on the preheated grill and cook for about 5-7 minutes per side, or until the fish is cooked through, and the skin is crispy. You can carefully flip the fish using a spatula.
While grilling, you can baste the branzino with any remaining marinade for added flavor.
Once done, transfer the grilled branzino to a serving platter.
Garnish with fresh herbs and serve hot.
Enjoy this Herb-infused Grilled Branzino with a side of roasted vegetables, couscous, or a simple green salad for a delightful Mediterranean-inspired meal.

**Tuscan Grilled Salmon with Balsamic Glaze**

Ingredients:

For the Salmon:

- 4 salmon fillets
- 1/4 cup extra-virgin olive oil
- 3 cloves garlic, minced
- 1 teaspoon dried oregano
- 1 teaspoon dried rosemary
- 1 teaspoon dried thyme
- Salt and black pepper, to taste
- Lemon wedges, for serving

For the Balsamic Glaze:

- 1/2 cup balsamic vinegar
- 2 tablespoons honey
- 1 teaspoon Dijon mustard
- Salt and black pepper, to taste

Instructions:

Preheat your grill to medium-high heat.
In a bowl, mix together olive oil, minced garlic, dried oregano, dried rosemary, dried thyme, salt, and black pepper to create the marinade for the salmon.
Pat the salmon fillets dry with paper towels and place them in a shallow dish. Brush the marinade over the fillets, ensuring they are well-coated. Allow the salmon to marinate for at least 30 minutes.
In a small saucepan, combine balsamic vinegar, honey, Dijon mustard, salt, and black pepper for the glaze. Bring the mixture to a simmer over medium heat, stirring frequently. Reduce the heat and simmer for about 5-7 minutes or until the glaze thickens. Remove from heat and set aside.
Grease the grill grates with a bit of oil to prevent sticking.
Place the salmon fillets on the preheated grill and cook for about 3-4 minutes per side, or until the fish is opaque and easily flakes with a fork.
While grilling, you can brush the salmon with any remaining marinade.
Once done, transfer the grilled salmon to a serving platter.
Drizzle the balsamic glaze over the grilled salmon fillets.
Serve the Tuscan Grilled Salmon with lemon wedges on the side.

Enjoy this flavorful salmon dish with a taste of Tuscany, pairing it with your favorite sides like roasted vegetables, risotto, or a simple green salad.

**Lebanese-style Grilled Cod with Sumac**

Ingredients:

- 4 cod fillets
- 1/4 cup olive oil
- 2 tablespoons fresh lemon juice
- 2 cloves garlic, minced
- 1 tablespoon ground sumac
- 1 teaspoon ground cumin
- 1 teaspoon ground coriander
- Salt and black pepper, to taste
- Fresh parsley, chopped, for garnish
- Lemon wedges, for serving

Instructions:

Preheat your grill to medium-high heat.
In a bowl, whisk together olive oil, fresh lemon juice, minced garlic, ground sumac, ground cumin, ground coriander, salt, and black pepper to create the marinade.
Pat the cod fillets dry with paper towels and place them in a shallow dish. Brush the marinade over the fillets, ensuring they are well-coated. Allow the cod to marinate for at least 30 minutes.
Grease the grill grates with a bit of oil to prevent sticking.
Place the cod fillets on the preheated grill and cook for about 3-4 minutes per side, or until the fish is opaque and easily flakes with a fork.
While grilling, you can brush the fillets with any remaining marinade for added flavor.
Once done, transfer the grilled cod to a serving platter.
Garnish with fresh chopped parsley and serve with lemon wedges on the side.
Enjoy this Lebanese-style Grilled Cod with Sumac with your favorite Lebanese or Mediterranean sides like tabbouleh, hummus, or roasted vegetables for a delicious and culturally inspired meal.

**Herb Crusted Grilled Sardines**

Ingredients:

- 8 fresh sardines, cleaned and gutted
- 1/4 cup olive oil
- 2 tablespoons fresh lemon juice
- 2 cloves garlic, minced
- 2 tablespoons fresh parsley, chopped
- 1 tablespoon fresh thyme leaves
- 1 teaspoon dried oregano
- Salt and black pepper, to taste
- Lemon wedges, for serving

Instructions:

Preheat your grill to medium-high heat.
In a bowl, whisk together olive oil, fresh lemon juice, minced garlic, chopped fresh parsley, fresh thyme leaves, dried oregano, salt, and black pepper to create the herb-infused marinade.
Pat the sardines dry with paper towels and place them in a shallow dish. Brush the marinade over the sardines, ensuring they are well-coated. Allow the sardines to marinate for at least 15-30 minutes.
Grease the grill grates with a bit of oil to prevent sticking.
Place the sardines on the preheated grill and cook for about 2-3 minutes per side, or until the fish is cooked through and has a nice grill mark.
While grilling, you can brush the sardines with any remaining marinade for added flavor.
Once done, transfer the grilled sardines to a serving platter.
Serve the Herb-Crusted Grilled Sardines hot, accompanied by lemon wedges on the side.
Enjoy these flavorful and nutritious sardines with a side of fresh salad, grilled vegetables, or crusty bread.

**Grilled Octopus with Mediterranean Marinade**

Ingredients:

- 2 pounds octopus, cleaned and tentacles separated
- 1/4 cup olive oil
- 3 tablespoons fresh lemon juice
- 2 cloves garlic, minced
- 1 teaspoon dried oregano
- 1 teaspoon dried thyme
- 1 teaspoon smoked paprika
- Salt and black pepper, to taste
- Lemon wedges, for serving
- Fresh parsley, chopped, for garnish

Instructions:

Preheat your grill to medium-high heat.
In a bowl, whisk together olive oil, fresh lemon juice, minced garlic, dried oregano, dried thyme, smoked paprika, salt, and black pepper to create the Mediterranean marinade.
Pat the octopus dry with paper towels and place it in a shallow dish. Brush the marinade over the octopus, ensuring it is well-coated. Allow the octopus to marinate for at least 30 minutes.
If the octopus is large, you may want to skewer it to make handling on the grill easier.
Grease the grill grates with a bit of oil to prevent sticking.
Place the octopus on the preheated grill and cook for about 3-4 minutes per side, or until it is cooked through and has a nice char.
While grilling, you can brush the octopus with any remaining marinade for added flavor.
Once done, transfer the grilled octopus to a serving platter.
Garnish with fresh chopped parsley and serve with lemon wedges on the side.
Enjoy this Grilled Octopus with Mediterranean Marinade as a delightful appetizer or part of a seafood feast with other Mediterranean-inspired dishes.

**Sicilian-style Grilled Grouper**

Ingredients:

- 4 grouper fillets (6-8 ounces each)
- 1/4 cup olive oil
- 2 tablespoons fresh lemon juice
- 3 cloves garlic, minced
- 2 tablespoons capers, drained
- 1/4 cup Kalamata olives, pitted and sliced
- 1 tablespoon fresh oregano, chopped (or 1 teaspoon dried oregano)
- 1 tablespoon fresh basil, chopped
- Salt and black pepper, to taste
- Lemon wedges, for serving

Instructions:

Preheat your grill to medium-high heat.
In a bowl, whisk together olive oil, fresh lemon juice, minced garlic, capers, sliced Kalamata olives, fresh oregano, fresh basil, salt, and black pepper to create the Sicilian-style marinade.
Pat the grouper fillets dry with paper towels and place them in a shallow dish. Pour the marinade over the fillets, ensuring they are well-coated. Marinate in the refrigerator for at least 30 minutes.
Grease the grill grates with a bit of oil to prevent sticking.
Place the grouper fillets on the preheated grill and cook for about 4-5 minutes per side, or until the fish is opaque and easily flakes with a fork.
While grilling, you can spoon some of the marinade over the fillets for added flavor.
Once done, transfer the grilled grouper to a serving platter.
Serve the Sicilian-style Grilled Grouper hot, garnished with additional fresh herbs, and with lemon wedges on the side.
Enjoy this flavorful and Mediterranean-inspired dish with a side of couscous, roasted vegetables, or a simple green salad.

**Turkish Yogurt-marinated Grilled Trout**

Ingredients:

- 4 whole trout, gutted and cleaned
- 1 cup plain Greek yogurt
- 3 tablespoons olive oil
- 2 tablespoons lemon juice
- 3 cloves garlic, minced
- 1 teaspoon ground cumin
- 1 teaspoon paprika
- 1 teaspoon dried oregano
- Salt and black pepper, to taste
- Fresh mint, chopped, for garnish
- Lemon wedges, for serving

Instructions:

In a bowl, combine Greek yogurt, olive oil, lemon juice, minced garlic, ground cumin, paprika, dried oregano, salt, and black pepper to create the marinade.

Pat the trout dry with paper towels and make a few diagonal cuts on each side of the fish to help the marinade penetrate.

Place the trout in a shallow dish and coat them evenly with the yogurt marinade. Make sure to get the marinade inside the cuts and cavity of the fish. Allow the trout to marinate in the refrigerator for at least 1-2 hours, or preferably overnight.

Preheat your grill to medium-high heat.

Grease the grill grates with a bit of oil to prevent sticking.

Remove the trout from the refrigerator and let them come to room temperature for about 10-15 minutes.

Place the trout on the preheated grill and cook for about 4-5 minutes per side, or until the fish is cooked through and has a nice grill mark.

While grilling, you can brush the trout with any remaining yogurt marinade for added flavor.

Once done, transfer the grilled trout to a serving platter.

Garnish with fresh chopped mint and serve with lemon wedges on the side.

Enjoy this Turkish Yogurt-Marinated Grilled Trout with a side of rice pilaf, grilled vegetables, or a refreshing cucumber salad for an authentic Turkish dining experience.

**Grilled Haddock with Tomato Caper Relish**

Ingredients:

For the Grilled Haddock:

- 4 haddock fillets
- 3 tablespoons olive oil
- 2 tablespoons fresh lemon juice
- 2 cloves garlic, minced
- 1 teaspoon dried thyme
- Salt and black pepper, to taste
- Lemon wedges, for serving

For the Tomato Caper Relish:

- 1 cup cherry tomatoes, quartered
- 2 tablespoons capers, drained
- 1/4 cup red onion, finely chopped
- 2 tablespoons fresh parsley, chopped
- 1 tablespoon fresh lemon juice
- 2 tablespoons extra-virgin olive oil
- Salt and black pepper, to taste

Instructions:

Preheat your grill to medium-high heat.
In a bowl, whisk together olive oil, fresh lemon juice, minced garlic, dried thyme, salt, and black pepper for the haddock marinade.
Pat the haddock fillets dry with paper towels and place them in a shallow dish. Brush the marinade over the fillets, ensuring they are well-coated. Marinate in the refrigerator for at least 30 minutes.
In a separate bowl, combine quartered cherry tomatoes, capers, finely chopped red onion, fresh parsley, fresh lemon juice, extra-virgin olive oil, salt, and black pepper to create the tomato caper relish. Set aside.
Grease the grill grates with a bit of oil to prevent sticking.
Place the marinated haddock fillets on the preheated grill and cook for about 3-4 minutes per side, or until the fish is opaque and easily flakes with a fork.
While grilling, you can brush the fillets with any remaining marinade for added flavor.

Once done, transfer the grilled haddock to a serving platter.
Spoon the tomato caper relish over the grilled haddock fillets.
Serve the Grilled Haddock with Tomato Caper Relish hot, accompanied by lemon wedges on the side.
Enjoy this delightful and light seafood dish with a side of quinoa, couscous, or steamed vegetables.

**Lemon Basil Grilled Hake**

Ingredients:

- 4 hake fillets
- 3 tablespoons olive oil
- 2 tablespoons fresh lemon juice
- 2 cloves garlic, minced
- 2 tablespoons fresh basil, chopped
- Zest of 1 lemon
- Salt and black pepper, to taste
- Lemon wedges, for serving

Instructions:

In a bowl, whisk together olive oil, fresh lemon juice, minced garlic, chopped fresh basil, lemon zest, salt, and black pepper to create the marinade.
Pat the hake fillets dry with paper towels and place them in a shallow dish. Brush the marinade over the fillets, ensuring they are well-coated. Marinate in the refrigerator for at least 30 minutes.
Preheat your grill to medium-high heat.
Grease the grill grates with a bit of oil to prevent sticking.
Place the marinated hake fillets on the preheated grill and cook for about 3-4 minutes per side, or until the fish is opaque and easily flakes with a fork.
While grilling, you can brush the fillets with any remaining marinade for added flavor.
Once done, transfer the grilled hake to a serving platter.
Serve the Lemon Basil Grilled Hake hot, accompanied by lemon wedges on the side.
Enjoy this light and flavorful dish with a side of couscous, quinoa, or a fresh green salad.

**Greek Souvlaki-inspired Grilled Whitefish**

Ingredients:

For the Marinade:

- 4 whitefish fillets (such as cod or haddock)
- 1/4 cup olive oil
- 3 tablespoons lemon juice
- 2 cloves garlic, minced
- 1 teaspoon dried oregano
- 1 teaspoon dried thyme
- Salt and black pepper, to taste

For the Tzatziki Sauce:

- 1 cup Greek yogurt
- 1/2 cucumber, grated and drained
- 2 cloves garlic, minced
- 1 tablespoon fresh dill, chopped
- 1 tablespoon fresh mint, chopped
- 1 tablespoon olive oil
- Salt and black pepper, to taste

For Serving:

- Pita bread
- Red onion, thinly sliced
- Tomato, sliced
- Fresh parsley, chopped
- Lemon wedges

Instructions:

In a bowl, whisk together olive oil, lemon juice, minced garlic, dried oregano, dried thyme, salt, and black pepper to create the marinade.

Pat the whitefish fillets dry with paper towels and place them in a shallow dish. Brush the marinade over the fillets, ensuring they are well-coated. Marinate in the refrigerator for at least 30 minutes.

Preheat your grill to medium-high heat.

In a separate bowl, prepare the tzatziki sauce by combining Greek yogurt, grated and drained cucumber, minced garlic, chopped fresh dill, chopped fresh mint, olive oil, salt, and black pepper. Mix well and refrigerate until serving.

Thread the marinated whitefish fillets onto skewers or use a grilling basket.

Grease the grill grates with a bit of oil to prevent sticking.

Grill the whitefish skewers for about 3-4 minutes per side, or until the fish is opaque and easily flakes with a fork.

While grilling, you can brush the fillets with any remaining marinade for added flavor.

Once done, remove the whitefish skewers from the grill.

Serve the grilled whitefish on pita bread, topped with sliced red onion, tomato, and a generous dollop of tzatziki sauce.

Garnish with chopped fresh parsley and serve with lemon wedges on the side.

Enjoy this Greek Souvlaki-inspired Grilled Whitefish as a delicious and light meal with Mediterranean flair.

**Mediterranean Stuffed Grilled Squid**

Ingredients:

For the Stuffed Squid:

- 8 small to medium-sized squid, cleaned and tentacles separated
- 1 cup cooked quinoa or rice
- 1/2 cup cherry tomatoes, halved
- 1/4 cup Kalamata olives, pitted and sliced
- 1/4 cup feta cheese, crumbled
- 2 tablespoons fresh parsley, chopped
- 2 cloves garlic, minced
- 2 tablespoons lemon juice
- 2 tablespoons olive oil
- Salt and black pepper, to taste

For the Grilling Marinade:

- 3 tablespoons olive oil
- 1 tablespoon lemon juice
- 1 teaspoon dried oregano
- Salt and black pepper, to taste

Instructions:

Preheat your grill to medium-high heat.
In a bowl, mix together cooked quinoa or rice, halved cherry tomatoes, sliced Kalamata olives, crumbled feta cheese, chopped fresh parsley, minced garlic, lemon juice, and olive oil for the stuffing. Season with salt and black pepper to taste.
Stuff each squid tube with the quinoa or rice mixture, leaving some space at the top to secure with toothpicks.
In a separate bowl, whisk together olive oil, lemon juice, dried oregano, salt, and black pepper to create the grilling marinade.
Brush the stuffed squids with the grilling marinade.
Skewer the stuffed squids or use a grilling basket to prevent them from falling through the grates.
Place the stuffed squids on the preheated grill and cook for about 3-4 minutes per side, or until the squid is cooked through and has a nice char.
While grilling, you can brush the squids with any remaining marinade.
Once done, transfer the grilled stuffed squids to a serving platter.
Serve the Mediterranean Stuffed Grilled Squid hot, accompanied by a side of lemon wedges.

Enjoy this delicious and flavorful dish as a main course or part of a Mediterranean feast.

**Grilled Tuna Nicoise Salad**

Ingredients:

For the Grilled Tuna:

- 4 tuna steaks (6-8 ounces each)
- 2 tablespoons olive oil
- 1 tablespoon Dijon mustard
- 2 cloves garlic, minced
- 1 teaspoon dried oregano
- Salt and black pepper, to taste
- Lemon wedges, for serving

For the Salad:

- 4 cups mixed salad greens (lettuce, arugula, spinach)
- 1 pound baby potatoes, boiled and halved
- 1 cup cherry tomatoes, halved
- 1 cup green beans, blanched and cut into bite-sized pieces
- 4 hard-boiled eggs, halved
- 1/2 cup Niçoise olives
- 1/4 cup capers, drained
- Fresh parsley, chopped, for garnish

For the Vinaigrette:

- 1/4 cup red wine vinegar
- 1/2 cup extra-virgin olive oil
- 1 tablespoon Dijon mustard
- 1 clove garlic, minced
- Salt and black pepper, to taste

Instructions:

In a bowl, whisk together olive oil, Dijon mustard, minced garlic, dried oregano, salt, and black pepper for the tuna marinade.
Pat the tuna steaks dry with paper towels and place them in a shallow dish.
Brush the marinade over the tuna steaks, ensuring they are well-coated. Marinate in the refrigerator for at least 30 minutes.

Preheat your grill to medium-high heat.

In a separate bowl, whisk together red wine vinegar, extra-virgin olive oil, Dijon mustard, minced garlic, salt, and black pepper to create the vinaigrette for the salad.

Grill the tuna steaks for about 2-3 minutes per side for medium-rare, or longer if you prefer your tuna more well-done. Remove from the grill and let them rest for a few minutes before slicing.

While the tuna is grilling, assemble the salad by arranging mixed greens, halved baby potatoes, cherry tomatoes, blanched green beans, hard-boiled eggs, Niçoise olives, and capers on a serving platter.

Slice the grilled tuna and place it on top of the salad.

Drizzle the vinaigrette over the Grilled Tuna Niçoise Salad.

Garnish with fresh chopped parsley and serve with lemon wedges on the side.

Enjoy this classic Niçoise Salad with the added twist of grilled tuna for a delicious and satisfying meal.

**Moroccan Harissa Grilled Catfish**

Ingredients:

For the Harissa Marinade:

- 2 tablespoons harissa paste
- 3 tablespoons olive oil
- 2 tablespoons fresh lemon juice
- 2 cloves garlic, minced
- 1 teaspoon ground cumin
- 1 teaspoon ground coriander
- 1 teaspoon smoked paprika
- Salt and black pepper, to taste

For the Catfish:

- 4 catfish fillets (6-8 ounces each)
- Lemon wedges, for serving
- Fresh cilantro, chopped, for garnish

Instructions:

In a bowl, whisk together harissa paste, olive oil, fresh lemon juice, minced garlic, ground cumin, ground coriander, smoked paprika, salt, and black pepper to create the harissa marinade.

Pat the catfish fillets dry with paper towels and place them in a shallow dish.

Brush the marinade over the catfish fillets, ensuring they are well-coated.

Marinate in the refrigerator for at least 30 minutes.

Preheat your grill to medium-high heat.

Grease the grill grates with a bit of oil to prevent sticking.

Place the marinated catfish fillets on the preheated grill and cook for about 3-4 minutes per side, or until the fish is opaque and easily flakes with a fork.

While grilling, you can brush the fillets with any remaining marinade for added flavor.

Once done, transfer the grilled catfish to a serving platter.

Serve the Moroccan Harissa Grilled Catfish hot, garnished with fresh chopped cilantro, and with lemon wedges on the side.

Enjoy this flavorful and spicy dish with a side of couscous, quinoa, or a simple green salad for a taste of Moroccan cuisine.

**Spanish Romesco Grilled Branzino**

Ingredients:

For the Romesco Sauce:

- 1 cup roasted red peppers, drained (from a jar or freshly roasted)
- 1/2 cup blanched almonds
- 2 cloves garlic, minced
- 1/4 cup extra-virgin olive oil
- 2 tablespoons tomato paste
- 2 tablespoons red wine vinegar
- 1 teaspoon smoked paprika
- Salt and black pepper, to taste

For the Grilled Branzino:

- 2 whole branzino, gutted and scaled
- 2 tablespoons olive oil
- Salt and black pepper, to taste
- Lemon wedges, for serving
- Fresh parsley, chopped, for garnish

Instructions:

For the Romesco Sauce:

In a food processor, combine roasted red peppers, blanched almonds, minced garlic, extra-virgin olive oil, tomato paste, red wine vinegar, smoked paprika, salt, and black pepper.
Process the ingredients until you achieve a smooth and thick sauce. Adjust seasoning to taste.
Transfer the Romesco sauce to a bowl and set aside.

For the Grilled Branzino:

Preheat your grill to medium-high heat.
Rinse the branzino under cold water and pat them dry with paper towels.
Rub the branzino with olive oil, both inside and out.

Season the branzino with salt and black pepper, ensuring that the seasoning is both inside the cavity and on the skin.

Grease the grill grates with a bit of oil to prevent sticking.

Place the branzino on the preheated grill and cook for about 4-5 minutes per side, or until the fish is cooked through, and the skin is crispy.

While grilling, you can brush the branzino with some olive oil for added moisture.

Once done, transfer the grilled branzino to a serving platter.

Serve the Spanish Romesco Grilled Branzino hot, accompanied by lemon wedges.

Drizzle the Romesco sauce over the branzino or serve it on the side.

Garnish with fresh chopped parsley.

Enjoy this Spanish-inspired dish with the rich flavors of Romesco sauce complementing the grilled branzino. Serve it with your favorite side dishes or a simple salad.

**Italian Lemon Rosemary Grilled Bass**

Ingredients:

- 4 bass fillets (about 6-8 ounces each)
- 1/4 cup olive oil
- 3 tablespoons fresh lemon juice
- 2 tablespoons fresh rosemary, finely chopped
- 2 cloves garlic, minced
- Zest of 1 lemon
- Salt and black pepper, to taste
- Lemon wedges, for serving
- Fresh rosemary sprigs, for garnish

Instructions:

In a bowl, whisk together olive oil, fresh lemon juice, finely chopped rosemary, minced garlic, lemon zest, salt, and black pepper to create the marinade.

Pat the bass fillets dry with paper towels and place them in a shallow dish. Brush the marinade over the fillets, ensuring they are well-coated. Marinate in the refrigerator for at least 30 minutes.

Preheat your grill to medium-high heat.

Grease the grill grates with a bit of oil to prevent sticking.

Place the marinated bass fillets on the preheated grill and cook for about 3-4 minutes per side, or until the fish is opaque and easily flakes with a fork.

While grilling, you can brush the fillets with any remaining marinade for added flavor.

Once done, transfer the grilled bass to a serving platter.

Serve the Italian Lemon Rosemary Grilled Bass hot, garnished with lemon wedges and fresh rosemary sprigs.

Enjoy this Italian-inspired dish with a side of roasted vegetables, risotto, or a light salad for a delicious and aromatic meal.

**Greek Yogurt Marinated Grilled Mullet**

Ingredients:

For the Greek Yogurt Marinade:

- 1 cup Greek yogurt
- 3 tablespoons olive oil
- 2 tablespoons fresh lemon juice
- 2 cloves garlic, minced
- 1 teaspoon dried oregano
- 1 teaspoon dried thyme
- Salt and black pepper, to taste

For the Grilled Mullet:

- 4 mullet fillets (about 6 ounces each)
- Lemon wedges, for serving
- Fresh parsley, chopped, for garnish

Instructions:

In a bowl, combine Greek yogurt, olive oil, fresh lemon juice, minced garlic, dried oregano, dried thyme, salt, and black pepper to create the marinade.
Pat the mullet fillets dry with paper towels and place them in a shallow dish. Brush the yogurt marinade over the fillets, ensuring they are well-coated. Marinate in the refrigerator for at least 30 minutes.
Preheat your grill to medium-high heat.
Grease the grill grates with a bit of oil to prevent sticking.
Place the marinated mullet fillets on the preheated grill and cook for about 3-4 minutes per side, or until the fish is opaque and easily flakes with a fork.
While grilling, you can brush the fillets with any remaining marinade for added flavor.
Once done, transfer the grilled mullet to a serving platter.
Serve the Greek Yogurt Marinated Grilled Mullet hot, accompanied by lemon wedges.
Garnish with freshly chopped parsley.
Enjoy this Greek-inspired dish with a side of Mediterranean rice, grilled vegetables, or a simple Greek salad for a light and flavorful meal.

**Grilled Swordfish with Mediterranean Salsa**

Ingredients:

For the Swordfish:

- 4 swordfish steaks (about 6-8 ounces each)
- 2 tablespoons olive oil
- 2 tablespoons fresh lemon juice
- 2 cloves garlic, minced
- 1 teaspoon dried oregano
- Salt and black pepper, to taste
- Lemon wedges, for serving

For the Mediterranean Salsa:

- 1 cup cherry tomatoes, quartered
- 1/2 cucumber, diced
- 1/4 cup red onion, finely chopped
- 1/4 cup Kalamata olives, pitted and sliced
- 2 tablespoons fresh parsley, chopped
- 2 tablespoons extra-virgin olive oil
- 1 tablespoon red wine vinegar
- Salt and black pepper, to taste

Instructions:

For the Swordfish:

In a bowl, whisk together olive oil, fresh lemon juice, minced garlic, dried oregano, salt, and black pepper to create the marinade.
Pat the swordfish steaks dry with paper towels and place them in a shallow dish. Brush the marinade over the steaks, ensuring they are well-coated. Marinate in the refrigerator for at least 30 minutes.
Preheat your grill to medium-high heat.
Grease the grill grates with a bit of oil to prevent sticking.
Place the marinated swordfish steaks on the preheated grill and cook for about 3-4 minutes per side, or until the fish is opaque and easily flakes with a fork.
While grilling, you can brush the steaks with any remaining marinade for added flavor.
Once done, transfer the grilled swordfish to a serving platter.

For the Mediterranean Salsa:

In a bowl, combine quartered cherry tomatoes, diced cucumber, finely chopped red onion, sliced Kalamata olives, chopped fresh parsley, extra-virgin olive oil, red wine vinegar, salt, and black pepper. Mix well.
Spoon the Mediterranean salsa over the grilled swordfish steaks.
Serve the Grilled Swordfish with Mediterranean Salsa hot, accompanied by lemon wedges on the side.
Enjoy this vibrant and delicious dish with a side of couscous, quinoa, or a simple green salad for a complete Mediterranean-inspired meal.

**Tunisian Spiced Grilled Tilapia**

Ingredients:

For the Tunisian Spice Rub:

- 1 teaspoon ground cumin
- 1 teaspoon ground coriander
- 1 teaspoon paprika
- 1/2 teaspoon ground cinnamon
- 1/2 teaspoon cayenne pepper (adjust to taste)
- 1 teaspoon ground turmeric
- Salt and black pepper, to taste

For the Grilled Tilapia:

- 4 tilapia fillets (about 6 ounces each)
- 2 tablespoons olive oil
- 2 tablespoons fresh lemon juice
- 2 cloves garlic, minced
- Lemon wedges, for serving
- Fresh cilantro, chopped, for garnish

Instructions:

In a small bowl, mix together ground cumin, ground coriander, paprika, ground cinnamon, cayenne pepper, ground turmeric, salt, and black pepper to create the Tunisian spice rub.
Pat the tilapia fillets dry with paper towels and rub the spice mixture evenly over both sides of each fillet. Press the spices into the fish to adhere.
In a separate bowl, whisk together olive oil, fresh lemon juice, and minced garlic.
Place the spiced tilapia fillets in a shallow dish and brush them with the olive oil and lemon juice mixture. Allow the fish to marinate for at least 15-30 minutes.
Preheat your grill to medium-high heat.
Grease the grill grates with a bit of oil to prevent sticking.
Place the marinated tilapia fillets on the preheated grill and cook for about 3-4 minutes per side, or until the fish is opaque and easily flakes with a fork.
While grilling, you can brush the fillets with any remaining marinade for added flavor.
Once done, transfer the grilled tilapia to a serving platter.
Serve the Tunisian Spiced Grilled Tilapia hot, garnished with fresh chopped cilantro, and with lemon wedges on the side.
Enjoy this flavorful and exotic dish with a side of couscous, roasted vegetables, or a simple green salad.

**Herb-infused Grilled Red Mullet**

Ingredients:

For the Herb Marinade:

- 1/4 cup olive oil
- 2 tablespoons fresh lemon juice
- 2 cloves garlic, minced
- 2 tablespoons fresh parsley, chopped
- 1 tablespoon fresh thyme leaves
- 1 teaspoon dried oregano
- Salt and black pepper, to taste

For the Grilled Red Mullet:

- 4 whole red mullet, scaled and gutted
- Olive oil for brushing
- Lemon wedges, for serving
- Fresh herbs (parsley, thyme) for garnish

Instructions:

For the Herb Marinade:

In a bowl, whisk together olive oil, fresh lemon juice, minced garlic, chopped fresh parsley, fresh thyme leaves, dried oregano, salt, and black pepper to create the herb marinade.
Set aside a small portion of the marinade for basting during grilling.

For the Grilled Red Mullet:

Preheat your grill to medium-high heat.
Make a few diagonal cuts on each side of the red mullet to help the marinade penetrate.
Brush the red mullet with the herb marinade, ensuring it gets into the cuts and cavity of the fish. Marinate for at least 15-30 minutes.
Grease the grill grates with a bit of oil to prevent sticking.
Place the marinated red mullet on the preheated grill and cook for about 3-4 minutes per side, or until the fish is cooked through and has a nice grill mark.
While grilling, baste the red mullet with the reserved herb marinade for added flavor.
Once done, transfer the grilled red mullet to a serving platter.
Garnish with fresh herbs and serve hot, accompanied by lemon wedges on the side.

Enjoy this Herb-infused Grilled Red Mullet as a delightful and aromatic dish with a side of Mediterranean rice, grilled vegetables, or a crisp salad.

**Grilled Shrimp with Olive Tapenade**

Ingredients:

For the Shrimp Marinade:

- 1 pound large shrimp, peeled and deveined
- 2 tablespoons olive oil
- 2 cloves garlic, minced
- 1 tablespoon fresh lemon juice
- 1 teaspoon dried oregano
- Salt and black pepper, to taste

For the Olive Tapenade:

- 1 cup Kalamata olives, pitted
- 2 tablespoons capers, drained
- 2 cloves garlic, minced
- 2 tablespoons fresh parsley, chopped
- 1 tablespoon fresh lemon juice
- 3 tablespoons extra-virgin olive oil
- Salt and black pepper, to taste

For Grilling:

- Wooden or metal skewers (if using wooden, soak them in water for 30 minutes)
- Olive oil for brushing

Instructions:

For the Shrimp Marinade:

In a bowl, combine olive oil, minced garlic, fresh lemon juice, dried oregano, salt, and black pepper to create the shrimp marinade.
Add the peeled and deveined shrimp to the marinade, ensuring they are well-coated.
Marinate for at least 15-30 minutes.

For the Olive Tapenade:

In a food processor, combine pitted Kalamata olives, capers, minced garlic, chopped fresh parsley, fresh lemon juice, extra-virgin olive oil, salt, and black pepper.

Pulse the ingredients until they form a coarse paste. Adjust seasoning to taste.

For Grilling:

Preheat your grill to medium-high heat.

Thread the marinated shrimp onto skewers.

Brush the grill grates with olive oil to prevent sticking.

Grill the shrimp skewers for about 2-3 minutes per side, or until the shrimp turn pink and opaque.

While grilling, you can brush the shrimp with additional olive oil for added flavor.

Once done, transfer the grilled shrimp to a serving platter.

Spoon the olive tapenade over the grilled shrimp or serve it on the side.

Serve the Grilled Shrimp with Olive Tapenade hot, and enjoy as an appetizer or main course.

Optionally, garnish with additional chopped parsley and lemon wedges.

This dish pairs well with a side of couscous, grilled vegetables, or a fresh green salad.

**Lemon Za'atar Grilled Mackerel**

Ingredients:

For the Lemon Za'atar Marinade:

- 1/4 cup olive oil
- 2 tablespoons fresh lemon juice
- 2 teaspoons za'atar spice blend
- 1 teaspoon ground cumin
- 1 teaspoon ground coriander
- 2 cloves garlic, minced
- Salt and black pepper, to taste

For the Grilled Mackerel:

- 4 mackerel fillets
- Olive oil for brushing
- Lemon wedges, for serving
- Fresh parsley, chopped, for garnish

Instructions:

For the Lemon Za'atar Marinade:

In a bowl, whisk together olive oil, fresh lemon juice, za'atar spice blend, ground cumin, ground coriander, minced garlic, salt, and black pepper to create the marinade.
Set aside a small portion of the marinade for basting during grilling.

For the Grilled Mackerel:

Pat the mackerel fillets dry with paper towels.
Brush the mackerel fillets with the Lemon Za'atar marinade, ensuring they are well-coated. Marinate for at least 15-30 minutes.
Preheat your grill to medium-high heat.
Grease the grill grates with a bit of oil to prevent sticking.
Place the marinated mackerel fillets on the preheated grill and cook for about 3-4 minutes per side, or until the fish is cooked through and has a nice grill mark.
While grilling, baste the mackerel with the reserved marinade for added flavor.

Once done, transfer the grilled mackerel to a serving platter.
Drizzle any remaining marinade over the mackerel.
Serve the Lemon Za'atar Grilled Mackerel hot, garnished with fresh chopped parsley and accompanied by lemon wedges.
Enjoy this flavorful and aromatic dish with a side of couscous, quinoa, or a simple green salad.

**Mediterranean Grilled Gurnard with Fennel**

Ingredients:

For the Grilled Gurnard:

- 4 gurnard fillets
- 3 tablespoons olive oil
- 2 tablespoons fresh lemon juice
- 2 cloves garlic, minced
- 1 teaspoon dried oregano
- Salt and black pepper, to taste
- Lemon wedges, for serving
- Fresh parsley, chopped, for garnish

For the Fennel Salad:

- 1 fennel bulb, thinly sliced
- 1/2 red onion, thinly sliced
- 1/4 cup Kalamata olives, pitted and sliced
- 2 tablespoons fresh lemon juice
- 2 tablespoons extra-virgin olive oil
- Salt and black pepper, to taste

Instructions:

For the Grilled Gurnard:

In a bowl, whisk together olive oil, fresh lemon juice, minced garlic, dried oregano, salt, and black pepper to create the marinade.
Pat the gurnard fillets dry with paper towels and place them in a shallow dish. Brush the marinade over the fillets, ensuring they are well-coated. Marinate in the refrigerator for at least 30 minutes.
Preheat your grill to medium-high heat.
Grease the grill grates with a bit of oil to prevent sticking.
Place the marinated gurnard fillets on the preheated grill and cook for about 3-4 minutes per side, or until the fish is cooked through and has a nice grill mark.
While grilling, you can brush the fillets with any remaining marinade for added flavor.
Once done, transfer the grilled gurnard to a serving platter.

For the Fennel Salad:

In a bowl, combine thinly sliced fennel, thinly sliced red onion, sliced Kalamata olives, fresh lemon juice, extra-virgin olive oil, salt, and black pepper. Toss the ingredients until well combined.

Adjust salt and pepper to taste.

Serve the Grilled Gurnard with a generous portion of Fennel Salad on the side.

Garnish with fresh chopped parsley and lemon wedges.

Enjoy this Mediterranean-inspired dish with the bright and crisp flavors of grilled gurnard and fennel salad.

**Spanish-style Grilled Herring**

Ingredients:

- 4 whole herring, gutted and scaled
- 3 tablespoons olive oil
- 2 tablespoons fresh lemon juice
- 2 cloves garlic, minced
- 1 teaspoon smoked paprika
- 1 teaspoon dried oregano
- Salt and black pepper, to taste
- Lemon wedges, for serving
- Fresh parsley, chopped, for garnish

Instructions:

Preheat your grill to medium-high heat.
Rinse the herring under cold water and pat them dry with paper towels.
In a bowl, whisk together olive oil, fresh lemon juice, minced garlic, smoked paprika, dried oregano, salt, and black pepper to create the marinade.
Make a few diagonal cuts on each side of the herring to help the marinade penetrate.
Brush the herring with the marinade, ensuring it gets into the cuts and cavity of the fish.
Marinate for at least 15-30 minutes.
Grease the grill grates with a bit of oil to prevent sticking.
Place the marinated herring on the preheated grill and cook for about 4-5 minutes per side, or until the fish is cooked through and has a nice char.
While grilling, you can brush the herring with any remaining marinade for added flavor.
Once done, transfer the grilled herring to a serving platter.
Serve the Spanish-style Grilled Herring hot, garnished with fresh chopped parsley and accompanied by lemon wedges on the side.
Enjoy this delicious and flavorful dish with a side of roasted potatoes, crusty bread, or a simple green salad.

**Italian Balsamic Glazed Grilled Tuna**

Ingredients:

For the Balsamic Glaze:

- 1/2 cup balsamic vinegar
- 2 tablespoons honey
- 1 tablespoon Dijon mustard
- 2 cloves garlic, minced
- Salt and black pepper, to taste

For the Grilled Tuna:

- 4 tuna steaks (about 6-8 ounces each)
- 2 tablespoons olive oil
- 2 tablespoons Italian seasoning
- Salt and black pepper, to taste
- Lemon wedges, for serving
- Fresh basil, chopped, for garnish

Instructions:

For the Balsamic Glaze:

In a small saucepan, combine balsamic vinegar, honey, Dijon mustard, minced garlic, salt, and black pepper.
Bring the mixture to a simmer over medium heat, stirring occasionally.
Reduce the heat to low and simmer for 10-15 minutes, or until the glaze has thickened.
Remove from heat and set aside.

For the Grilled Tuna:

Preheat your grill to medium-high heat.
In a bowl, mix together olive oil, Italian seasoning, salt, and black pepper to create a marinade.
Pat the tuna steaks dry with paper towels and brush them with the marinade, ensuring they are well-coated. Let them marinate for about 15-30 minutes.
Grease the grill grates with a bit of oil to prevent sticking.
Place the marinated tuna steaks on the preheated grill and cook for about 2-3 minutes per side for medium-rare, or longer if you prefer your tuna more well-done.

While grilling, you can brush the tuna steaks with the balsamic glaze for added flavor.
Once done, transfer the grilled tuna to a serving platter.
Drizzle the remaining balsamic glaze over the tuna steaks.
Serve the Italian Balsamic Glazed Grilled Tuna hot, garnished with chopped fresh basil and accompanied by lemon wedges.
Enjoy this delicious and elegant dish with a side of roasted vegetables, couscous, or a green salad.

**Grilled Mediterranean Bluefish with Herbs**

Ingredients:

For the Herb Marinade:

- 1/4 cup olive oil
- 2 tablespoons fresh lemon juice
- 2 cloves garlic, minced
- 2 tablespoons fresh parsley, chopped
- 1 tablespoon fresh oregano, chopped
- 1 tablespoon fresh thyme leaves
- Salt and black pepper, to taste

For the Grilled Bluefish:

- 4 bluefish fillets (about 6-8 ounces each)
- Lemon wedges, for serving
- Fresh herbs (parsley, oregano, thyme) for garnish

Instructions:

For the Herb Marinade:

In a bowl, whisk together olive oil, fresh lemon juice, minced garlic, chopped fresh parsley, chopped fresh oregano, chopped fresh thyme, salt, and black pepper to create the herb marinade.
Set aside a small portion of the marinade for basting during grilling.

For the Grilled Bluefish:

Pat the bluefish fillets dry with paper towels.
Brush the bluefish fillets with the Herb Marinade, ensuring they are well-coated. Marinate for at least 15-30 minutes.
Preheat your grill to medium-high heat.
Grease the grill grates with a bit of oil to prevent sticking.
Place the marinated bluefish fillets on the preheated grill and cook for about 4-5 minutes per side, or until the fish is cooked through and has a nice grill mark.
While grilling, baste the bluefish fillets with the reserved marinade for added flavor.
Once done, transfer the grilled bluefish to a serving platter.
Garnish with fresh herbs and serve hot, accompanied by lemon wedges on the side.

Enjoy this Grilled Mediterranean Bluefish with Herbs as a flavorful and nutritious dish. Pair it with a side of roasted vegetables, quinoa, or a simple green salad for a complete meal.

**Herb Crusted Grilled Cuttlefish**

Ingredients:

For the Herb Crust:

- 1/4 cup breadcrumbs
- 2 tablespoons fresh parsley, chopped
- 1 tablespoon fresh cilantro, chopped
- 1 tablespoon fresh mint, chopped
- 1 tablespoon fresh lemon zest
- 2 cloves garlic, minced
- 2 tablespoons olive oil
- Salt and black pepper, to taste

For the Grilled Cuttlefish:

- 2 medium-sized cuttlefish, cleaned and scored
- 2 tablespoons olive oil
- 2 tablespoons fresh lemon juice
- Salt and black pepper, to taste
- Lemon wedges, for serving

Instructions:

For the Herb Crust:

In a bowl, combine breadcrumbs, chopped fresh parsley, chopped fresh cilantro, chopped fresh mint, minced garlic, fresh lemon zest, olive oil, salt, and black pepper. Mix well to form the herb crust.

For the Grilled Cuttlefish:

Preheat your grill to medium-high heat.
In a separate bowl, whisk together olive oil and fresh lemon juice.
Pat the cleaned and scored cuttlefish dry with paper towels.
Brush the cuttlefish with the olive oil and lemon juice mixture, ensuring they are well-coated.
Season the cuttlefish with salt and black pepper.
Press the herb crust onto both sides of the cuttlefish, ensuring an even coating.
Grease the grill grates with a bit of oil to prevent sticking.

Place the herb-crusted cuttlefish on the preheated grill and cook for about 2-3 minutes per side, or until the cuttlefish is cooked through and has a nice grill mark.
Once done, transfer the grilled cuttlefish to a serving platter.
Serve the Herb-Crusted Grilled Cuttlefish hot, accompanied by lemon wedges on the side. Enjoy this unique and flavorful dish as an appetizer or part of a seafood feast. You can also pair it with a fresh green salad or a side of grilled vegetables.

**Turkish Spiced Grilled Sea Bass**

Ingredients:

For the Turkish Spice Blend:

- 1 tablespoon ground cumin
- 1 tablespoon ground coriander
- 1 tablespoon smoked paprika
- 1 teaspoon ground cinnamon
- 1 teaspoon ground cayenne pepper (adjust to taste)
- 1 teaspoon ground sumac
- Salt and black pepper, to taste

For the Grilled Sea Bass:

- 4 sea bass fillets (about 6-8 ounces each)
- 3 tablespoons olive oil
- 2 tablespoons fresh lemon juice
- 2 cloves garlic, minced
- Turkish spice blend (from above)
- Salt, to taste
- Lemon wedges, for serving
- Fresh parsley, chopped, for garnish

Instructions:

For the Turkish Spice Blend:

In a small bowl, mix together ground cumin, ground coriander, smoked paprika, ground cinnamon, ground cayenne pepper, ground sumac, salt, and black pepper to create the Turkish spice blend.

For the Grilled Sea Bass:

Pat the sea bass fillets dry with paper towels.
In a bowl, whisk together olive oil, fresh lemon juice, minced garlic, and a generous amount of the Turkish spice blend.
Place the sea bass fillets in a shallow dish and brush them with the spice-infused olive oil mixture, ensuring they are well-coated. Marinate in the refrigerator for at least 30 minutes.
Preheat your grill to medium-high heat.

Grease the grill grates with a bit of oil to prevent sticking.

Place the marinated sea bass fillets on the preheated grill and cook for about 3-4 minutes per side, or until the fish is opaque and easily flakes with a fork.

While grilling, you can brush the fillets with any remaining spice-infused olive oil for added flavor.

Once done, transfer the grilled sea bass to a serving platter.

Serve the Turkish Spiced Grilled Sea Bass hot, garnished with chopped fresh parsley and accompanied by lemon wedges on the side.

Enjoy this flavorful and aromatic dish with a side of couscous, roasted vegetables, or a refreshing salad for a taste of Turkish cuisine.

**Grilled Branzino with Lemon Caper Sauce**

Ingredients:

For the Grilled Branzino:

- 2 whole branzino, gutted and scaled
- 3 tablespoons olive oil
- 2 cloves garlic, minced
- 1 tablespoon fresh lemon juice
- Salt and black pepper, to taste
- Lemon slices, for garnish
- Fresh parsley, chopped, for garnish

For the Lemon Caper Sauce:

- 1/4 cup unsalted butter
- 2 tablespoons capers, drained
- 2 tablespoons fresh lemon juice
- 1 tablespoon fresh parsley, chopped
- Salt and black pepper, to taste

Instructions:

For the Grilled Branzino:

Preheat your grill to medium-high heat.
Rinse the branzino under cold water and pat them dry with paper towels.
In a small bowl, mix together olive oil, minced garlic, fresh lemon juice, salt, and black pepper to create a marinade.
Make a few diagonal cuts on each side of the branzino to help the marinade penetrate.
Brush the branzino with the marinade, ensuring it gets into the cuts and cavity of the fish.
Marinate for at least 15-30 minutes.
Grease the grill grates with a bit of oil to prevent sticking.
Place the marinated branzino on the preheated grill and cook for about 4-5 minutes per side, or until the fish is cooked through and has a nice grill mark.
While grilling, you can brush the branzino with any remaining marinade for added flavor.
Once done, transfer the grilled branzino to a serving platter.

For the Lemon Caper Sauce:

In a small saucepan, melt the butter over medium heat.
Add capers, fresh lemon juice, and chopped parsley to the melted butter. Stir well.
Season the sauce with salt and black pepper to taste.
Allow the sauce to simmer for a few minutes until it thickens slightly.
Pour the lemon caper sauce over the grilled branzino.
Garnish with lemon slices and chopped fresh parsley.
Serve the Grilled Branzino with Lemon Caper Sauce hot, and enjoy the combination of grilled fish with the zesty and briny flavors of the sauce.

**Moroccan Charmoula Grilled Mackerel**

Ingredients:

For the Charmoula Marinade:

- 1/4 cup fresh cilantro, chopped
- 1/4 cup fresh parsley, chopped
- 2 cloves garlic, minced
- 1 teaspoon ground cumin
- 1 teaspoon ground coriander
- 1 teaspoon paprika
- 1/2 teaspoon ground cayenne pepper (adjust to taste)
- 1/4 cup olive oil
- 2 tablespoons fresh lemon juice
- Salt and black pepper, to taste

For the Grilled Mackerel:

- 4 mackerel fillets
- Olive oil for brushing
- Lemon wedges, for serving
- Fresh cilantro, chopped, for garnish

Instructions:

For the Charmoula Marinade:

In a food processor or blender, combine chopped cilantro, chopped parsley, minced garlic, ground cumin, ground coriander, paprika, ground cayenne pepper, olive oil, fresh lemon juice, salt, and black pepper.
Blend the ingredients until you achieve a smooth and vibrant marinade.

For the Grilled Mackerel:

Pat the mackerel fillets dry with paper towels.
Generously brush the mackerel fillets with the Charmoula marinade, ensuring they are well-coated. Marinate for at least 30 minutes, allowing the flavors to infuse.
Preheat your grill to medium-high heat.

Grease the grill grates with a bit of oil to prevent sticking.
Place the marinated mackerel fillets on the preheated grill and cook for about 3-4 minutes per side, or until the fish is cooked through and has a nice grill mark.
While grilling, you can brush the fillets with any remaining Charmoula marinade for added flavor.
Once done, transfer the grilled mackerel to a serving platter.
Serve the Moroccan Charmoula Grilled Mackerel hot, garnished with fresh chopped cilantro and accompanied by lemon wedges on the side.
Enjoy this Moroccan-inspired dish with a side of couscous, quinoa, or a light salad for a delightful and flavorful meal.

**Greek Feta-stuffed Grilled Anchovies**

Ingredients:

For the Feta Stuffing:

- 1/2 cup crumbled feta cheese
- 2 tablespoons fresh parsley, chopped
- 1 tablespoon lemon zest
- 1 tablespoon olive oil
- 1 clove garlic, minced
- Black pepper, to taste

For the Grilled Anchovies:

- 12 fresh anchovies, cleaned and butterflied (or use deboned fillets)
- Olive oil for brushing
- Lemon wedges, for serving
- Fresh parsley, chopped, for garnish

Instructions:

For the Feta Stuffing:

In a bowl, combine crumbled feta cheese, chopped fresh parsley, lemon zest, olive oil, minced garlic, and black pepper. Mix well to create the feta stuffing.

For the Grilled Anchovies:

Preheat your grill to medium-high heat.
If you have whole anchovies, clean and butterfly them by removing the backbone and spreading the fish open. If using fillets, ensure they are deboned.
Spoon the feta stuffing onto each anchovy or fillet, and then fold them over to encase the stuffing.
Secure the stuffed anchovies with toothpicks to keep them closed during grilling.
Brush the stuffed anchovies with olive oil to prevent sticking and enhance flavor.
Place the stuffed anchovies on the preheated grill and cook for about 2-3 minutes per side, or until the fish is cooked through and has a nice grill mark.
While grilling, you can brush the anchovies with additional olive oil for added flavor.
Once done, transfer the grilled feta-stuffed anchovies to a serving platter.

Serve the Greek Feta-stuffed Grilled Anchovies hot, garnished with fresh chopped parsley and accompanied by lemon wedges on the side.

Enjoy this Greek-inspired dish as a delightful appetizer or part of a seafood feast. Pair it with a side of Greek salad, olives, or crusty bread for a complete Mediterranean experience.

**Sicilian-style Grilled Amberjack**

Ingredients:

For the Sicilian Marinade:

- 1/4 cup extra-virgin olive oil
- 2 tablespoons fresh lemon juice
- 2 cloves garlic, minced
- 2 tablespoons fresh parsley, chopped
- 1 tablespoon capers, drained and chopped
- 1 tablespoon green olives, pitted and chopped
- 1 teaspoon dried oregano
- Salt and black pepper, to taste

For the Grilled Amberjack:

- 4 amberjack fillets (about 6-8 ounces each)
- Olive oil for brushing
- Lemon wedges, for serving
- Fresh parsley, chopped, for garnish

Instructions:

For the Sicilian Marinade:

In a bowl, whisk together extra-virgin olive oil, fresh lemon juice, minced garlic, chopped fresh parsley, chopped capers, chopped green olives, dried oregano, salt, and black pepper to create the Sicilian marinade.

For the Grilled Amberjack:

Pat the amberjack fillets dry with paper towels.
Place the amberjack fillets in a shallow dish and brush them with the Sicilian marinade, ensuring they are well-coated. Marinate for at least 30 minutes, allowing the flavors to infuse.
Preheat your grill to medium-high heat.
Grease the grill grates with a bit of oil to prevent sticking.
Place the marinated amberjack fillets on the preheated grill and cook for about 3-4 minutes per side, or until the fish is cooked through and has a nice grill mark.
While grilling, you can brush the fillets with any remaining Sicilian marinade for added flavor.
Once done, transfer the grilled amberjack to a serving platter.

Serve the Sicilian-style Grilled Amberjack hot, garnished with fresh chopped parsley and accompanied by lemon wedges on the side.

Enjoy this flavorful and Mediterranean-inspired dish with a side of roasted vegetables, couscous, or a simple green salad.

**Lemon Garlic Grilled John Dory**

Ingredients:

For the Lemon Garlic Marinade:

- 1/4 cup olive oil
- 3 tablespoons fresh lemon juice
- Zest of 1 lemon
- 3 cloves garlic, minced
- 1 tablespoon fresh parsley, chopped
- Salt and black pepper, to taste

For the Grilled John Dory:

- 4 John Dory fillets (about 6-8 ounces each)
- Olive oil for brushing
- Lemon wedges, for serving
- Fresh parsley, chopped, for garnish

Instructions:

For the Lemon Garlic Marinade:

In a bowl, whisk together olive oil, fresh lemon juice, lemon zest, minced garlic, chopped fresh parsley, salt, and black pepper to create the marinade.

For the Grilled John Dory:

Pat the John Dory fillets dry with paper towels.
Place the John Dory fillets in a shallow dish and brush them with the Lemon Garlic marinade, ensuring they are well-coated. Marinate for at least 15-30 minutes.
Preheat your grill to medium-high heat.
Grease the grill grates with a bit of oil to prevent sticking.
Place the marinated John Dory fillets on the preheated grill and cook for about 3-4 minutes per side, or until the fish is cooked through and has a nice grill mark.
While grilling, you can brush the fillets with any remaining Lemon Garlic marinade for added flavor.
Once done, transfer the grilled John Dory to a serving platter.

Serve the Lemon Garlic Grilled John Dory hot, garnished with fresh chopped parsley and accompanied by lemon wedges on the side.

Enjoy this light and flavorful dish with a side of quinoa, steamed vegetables, or a simple salad for a complete meal.

**Italian Pesto Grilled Red Snapper**

Ingredients:

For the Pesto Marinade:

- 1 cup fresh basil leaves, packed
- 1/2 cup grated Parmesan cheese
- 1/4 cup pine nuts
- 3 cloves garlic, minced
- 1/2 cup extra-virgin olive oil
- Salt and black pepper, to taste

For the Grilled Red Snapper:

- 4 red snapper fillets (about 6-8 ounces each)
- Olive oil for brushing
- Lemon wedges, for serving
- Fresh basil, chopped, for garnish

Instructions:

For the Pesto Marinade:

> In a food processor, combine fresh basil, grated Parmesan cheese, pine nuts, and minced garlic.
> Pulse the ingredients until finely chopped.
> With the food processor running, slowly pour in the olive oil until the mixture forms a smooth pesto sauce.
> Season the pesto with salt and black pepper to taste. Set aside.

For the Grilled Red Snapper:

> Pat the red snapper fillets dry with paper towels.
> Brush both sides of each fillet with the Pesto Marinade, ensuring they are well-coated. Reserve a small amount of pesto for serving.
> Marinate the red snapper fillets for at least 15-30 minutes.
> Preheat your grill to medium-high heat.
> Grease the grill grates with a bit of oil to prevent sticking.

Place the marinated red snapper fillets on the preheated grill and cook for about 3-4 minutes per side, or until the fish is cooked through and has a nice grill mark. While grilling, you can brush the fillets with any remaining pesto for added flavor.
Once done, transfer the grilled red snapper to a serving platter.
Drizzle the reserved pesto over the fillets.
Serve the Italian Pesto Grilled Red Snapper hot, garnished with fresh chopped basil and accompanied by lemon wedges on the side.
Enjoy this delicious and vibrant dish with a side of pasta, roasted vegetables, or a light salad.

**Grilled Sardine Skewers with Lemon**

Ingredients:

- 12 fresh sardines, cleaned and gutted
- Olive oil for brushing
- Salt and black pepper, to taste
- Zest of 1 lemon
- Lemon wedges, for serving
- Fresh parsley, chopped, for garnish

Instructions:

Preheat your grill to medium-high heat.
Rinse the sardines under cold water and pat them dry with paper towels.
Thread the sardines onto skewers, making sure to secure them so they don't fall apart during grilling.
Brush the sardine skewers with olive oil, ensuring they are well-coated.
Season the skewers with salt and black pepper to taste.
Place the sardine skewers on the preheated grill and cook for about 2-3 minutes per side, or until the fish is cooked through and has a nice grill mark.
While grilling, sprinkle the lemon zest over the sardine skewers for added flavor.
Once done, transfer the grilled sardine skewers to a serving platter.
Garnish with chopped fresh parsley and serve hot, accompanied by lemon wedges on the side.
Enjoy these Grilled Sardine Skewers with Lemon as a delicious appetizer or part of a Mediterranean-inspired meal. Serve with crusty bread or a simple salad for a light and flavorful dish.

**Spanish Romesco Grilled Mullet**

Ingredients:

For the Romesco Sauce:

- 1 cup roasted red bell peppers, peeled and chopped
- 1/2 cup blanched almonds
- 2 cloves garlic, minced
- 2 tablespoons tomato paste
- 2 tablespoons red wine vinegar
- 1 teaspoon smoked paprika
- 1/2 teaspoon cayenne pepper (adjust to taste)
- 1/2 cup extra-virgin olive oil
- Salt and black pepper, to taste

For the Grilled Mullet:

- 4 mullet fillets (about 6-8 ounces each)
- Olive oil for brushing
- Lemon wedges, for serving
- Fresh parsley, chopped, for garnish

Instructions:

For the Romesco Sauce:

In a food processor or blender, combine roasted red bell peppers, blanched almonds, minced garlic, tomato paste, red wine vinegar, smoked paprika, cayenne pepper, salt, and black pepper.
Pulse the ingredients until a coarse paste forms.
With the processor running, slowly drizzle in the olive oil until the sauce reaches your desired consistency. Adjust salt and pepper to taste.

For the Grilled Mullet:

Preheat your grill to medium-high heat.
Pat the mullet fillets dry with paper towels.
Brush both sides of each fillet with olive oil to prevent sticking.
Place the mullet fillets on the preheated grill and cook for about 3-4 minutes per side, or until the fish is cooked through and has a nice grill mark.

While grilling, you can brush the fillets with additional olive oil for added flavor.

Once done, transfer the grilled mullet to a serving platter.

Spoon the Romesco Sauce over the mullet fillets.

Garnish with chopped fresh parsley and serve hot, accompanied by lemon wedges on the side.

Enjoy this Spanish Romesco Grilled Mullet with its rich, nutty, and smoky flavors. Serve it with a side of sautéed vegetables, rice, or crusty bread.

**Mediterranean Grilled Mackinaw with Tomato**

Ingredients:

- 4 Mackinaw trout fillets (about 6-8 ounces each)
- Olive oil for brushing
- Salt and black pepper, to taste
- 2 teaspoons dried oregano
- 2 teaspoons dried thyme
- 1 teaspoon smoked paprika
- 2 cloves garlic, minced
- 2 cups cherry tomatoes, halved
- Fresh parsley, chopped, for garnish
- Lemon wedges, for serving

Instructions:

Preheat your grill to medium-high heat.
Pat the Mackinaw trout fillets dry with paper towels.
In a small bowl, mix together olive oil, salt, black pepper, dried oregano, dried thyme, smoked paprika, and minced garlic to create a marinade.
Brush the Mackinaw trout fillets with the marinade, ensuring they are well-coated. Let them marinate for about 15-30 minutes.
In the meantime, prepare the cherry tomatoes by halving them.
Grease the grill grates with a bit of oil to prevent sticking.
Place the marinated Mackinaw trout fillets on the preheated grill and cook for about 4-5 minutes per side, or until the fish is cooked through and has a nice grill mark.
While grilling, you can brush the fillets with any remaining marinade for added flavor.
In the last 2 minutes of grilling, add the halved cherry tomatoes to the grill, just until they start to soften and get grill marks.
Once done, transfer the grilled Mackinaw fillets to a serving platter and scatter the grilled tomatoes over them.
Garnish with chopped fresh parsley and serve hot, accompanied by lemon wedges on the side.
Enjoy this Mediterranean Grilled Mackinaw with Tomato, featuring the flavors of herbs, spices, and grilled tomatoes for a delightful meal. Pair it with a side of quinoa, couscous, or a fresh green salad.

**Lebanese Sumac Grilled Porgy**

Ingredients:

For the Sumac Marinade:

- 1/4 cup olive oil
- 2 tablespoons ground sumac
- 1 tablespoon ground cumin
- 1 tablespoon ground coriander
- 2 cloves garlic, minced
- 2 tablespoons fresh lemon juice
- Salt and black pepper, to taste

For the Grilled Porgy:

- 4 whole porgy, cleaned and scaled
- Olive oil for brushing
- Lemon wedges, for serving
- Fresh parsley, chopped, for garnish

Instructions:

For the Sumac Marinade:

In a bowl, whisk together olive oil, ground sumac, ground cumin, ground coriander, minced garlic, fresh lemon juice, salt, and black pepper to create the sumac marinade.

For the Grilled Porgy:

Rinse the porgy under cold water and pat them dry with paper towels.
Make a few diagonal cuts on each side of the porgy to help the marinade penetrate.
Brush the porgy with the sumac marinade, ensuring it gets into the cuts and cavity of the fish. Marinate for at least 30 minutes.
Preheat your grill to medium-high heat.
Grease the grill grates with a bit of oil to prevent sticking.
Place the marinated porgy on the preheated grill and cook for about 5-6 minutes per side, or until the fish is cooked through and has a nice grill mark.
While grilling, you can brush the porgy with any remaining sumac marinade for added flavor.
Once done, transfer the grilled porgy to a serving platter.

Serve the Lebanese Sumac Grilled Porgy hot, garnished with fresh chopped parsley and accompanied by lemon wedges on the side.

Enjoy this Lebanese-inspired dish with a side of tabbouleh, rice, or grilled vegetables for a flavorful and aromatic meal.

**Greek-style Grilled Yellowtail**

Ingredients:

For the Greek Marinade:

- 1/4 cup extra-virgin olive oil
- 2 tablespoons fresh lemon juice
- 2 cloves garlic, minced
- 1 teaspoon dried oregano
- 1 teaspoon dried thyme
- 1 teaspoon paprika
- Salt and black pepper, to taste

For the Grilled Yellowtail:

- 4 yellowtail fillets (about 6-8 ounces each)
- Olive oil for brushing
- Lemon wedges, for serving
- Fresh parsley, chopped, for garnish

Instructions:

For the Greek Marinade:

In a bowl, whisk together extra-virgin olive oil, fresh lemon juice, minced garlic, dried oregano, dried thyme, paprika, salt, and black pepper to create the Greek marinade.

For the Grilled Yellowtail:

Pat the yellowtail fillets dry with paper towels.
Brush both sides of each fillet with olive oil to prevent sticking.
Place the yellowtail fillets in a shallow dish and brush them with the Greek marinade, ensuring they are well-coated. Marinate for at least 15-30 minutes.
Preheat your grill to medium-high heat.
Grease the grill grates with a bit of oil to prevent sticking.
Place the marinated yellowtail fillets on the preheated grill and cook for about 3-4 minutes per side, or until the fish is cooked through and has a nice grill mark.

While grilling, you can brush the fillets with any remaining Greek marinade for added flavor.

Once done, transfer the grilled yellowtail to a serving platter.

Serve the Greek-style Grilled Yellowtail hot, garnished with fresh chopped parsley and accompanied by lemon wedges on the side.

Enjoy this Greek-inspired dish with a side of Greek salad, roasted potatoes, or orzo for a complete and delicious meal.

**Tuscan Herb Grilled Rainbow Trout**

Ingredients:

For the Tuscan Herb Marinade:

- 1/4 cup extra-virgin olive oil
- 2 tablespoons balsamic vinegar
- 2 cloves garlic, minced
- 1 teaspoon dried rosemary
- 1 teaspoon dried thyme
- 1 teaspoon dried oregano
- Salt and black pepper, to taste

For the Grilled Rainbow Trout:

- 4 rainbow trout fillets (about 6-8 ounces each)
- Olive oil for brushing
- Lemon wedges, for serving
- Fresh parsley, chopped, for garnish

Instructions:

For the Tuscan Herb Marinade:

In a bowl, whisk together extra-virgin olive oil, balsamic vinegar, minced garlic, dried rosemary, dried thyme, dried oregano, salt, and black pepper to create the Tuscan herb marinade.

For the Grilled Rainbow Trout:

Pat the rainbow trout fillets dry with paper towels.
Brush both sides of each fillet with olive oil to prevent sticking.
Place the rainbow trout fillets in a shallow dish and brush them with the Tuscan herb marinade, ensuring they are well-coated. Marinate for at least 15-30 minutes.
Preheat your grill to medium-high heat.
Grease the grill grates with a bit of oil to prevent sticking.
Place the marinated rainbow trout fillets on the preheated grill and cook for about 3-4 minutes per side, or until the fish is cooked through and has a nice grill mark.
While grilling, you can brush the fillets with any remaining Tuscan herb marinade for added flavor.

Once done, transfer the grilled rainbow trout to a serving platter.
Serve the Tuscan Herb Grilled Rainbow Trout hot, garnished with fresh chopped parsley and accompanied by lemon wedges on the side.
Enjoy this flavorful and herby dish with a side of roasted vegetables, couscous, or a light salad for a taste of Tuscany.

**Moroccan Ras el Hanout Grilled Perch**

Ingredients:

For the Ras el Hanout Marinade:

- 1/4 cup olive oil
- 2 tablespoons fresh lemon juice
- 2 teaspoons Ras el Hanout spice blend
- 1 teaspoon ground cumin
- 1 teaspoon ground coriander
- 1 teaspoon paprika
- 2 cloves garlic, minced
- Salt and black pepper, to taste

For the Grilled Perch:

- 4 perch fillets (about 6-8 ounces each)
- Olive oil for brushing
- Lemon wedges, for serving
- Fresh cilantro, chopped, for garnish

Instructions:

For the Ras el Hanout Marinade:

In a bowl, whisk together olive oil, fresh lemon juice, Ras el Hanout spice blend, ground cumin, ground coriander, paprika, minced garlic, salt, and black pepper to create the marinade.

For the Grilled Perch:

Pat the perch fillets dry with paper towels.
Brush both sides of each fillet with olive oil to prevent sticking.
Place the perch fillets in a shallow dish and brush them with the Ras el Hanout marinade, ensuring they are well-coated. Marinate for at least 15-30 minutes.
Preheat your grill to medium-high heat.
Grease the grill grates with a bit of oil to prevent sticking.
Place the marinated perch fillets on the preheated grill and cook for about 3-4 minutes per side, or until the fish is cooked through and has a nice grill mark.

While grilling, you can brush the fillets with any remaining Ras el Hanout marinade for added flavor.
Once done, transfer the grilled perch to a serving platter.
Serve the Moroccan Ras el Hanout Grilled Perch hot, garnished with fresh chopped cilantro and accompanied by lemon wedges on the side.
Enjoy this aromatic and spicy dish with couscous, rice, or a side of roasted vegetables for a taste of Moroccan cuisine.

**Grilled Sea Bream with Mediterranean Vinaigrette**

Ingredients:

For the Mediterranean Vinaigrette:

- 1/4 cup extra-virgin olive oil
- 2 tablespoons red wine vinegar
- 1 tablespoon Dijon mustard
- 1 clove garlic, minced
- 1 teaspoon dried oregano
- 1 teaspoon dried thyme
- Salt and black pepper, to taste

For the Grilled Sea Bream:

- 4 sea bream fillets (about 6-8 ounces each)
- Olive oil for brushing
- Lemon wedges, for serving
- Fresh basil, chopped, for garnish

Instructions:

For the Mediterranean Vinaigrette:

In a small bowl, whisk together extra-virgin olive oil, red wine vinegar, Dijon mustard, minced garlic, dried oregano, dried thyme, salt, and black pepper to create the Mediterranean vinaigrette. Set aside.

For the Grilled Sea Bream:

Pat the sea bream fillets dry with paper towels.
Brush both sides of each fillet with olive oil to prevent sticking.
Preheat your grill to medium-high heat.
Grease the grill grates with a bit of oil to prevent sticking.
Place the sea bream fillets on the preheated grill and cook for about 3-4 minutes per side, or until the fish is cooked through and has a nice grill mark.
While grilling, you can brush the fillets with any remaining Mediterranean vinaigrette for added flavor.
Once done, transfer the grilled sea bream to a serving platter.
Drizzle the Mediterranean vinaigrette over the fillets.

Serve the Grilled Sea Bream with Mediterranean Vinaigrette hot, garnished with fresh chopped basil and accompanied by lemon wedges on the side.
Enjoy this light and flavorful dish with a side of couscous, roasted vegetables, or a fresh green salad for a taste of the Mediterranean.

**Italian Herb Grilled Mahi-Mahi**

Ingredients:

For the Italian Herb Marinade:

- 1/4 cup extra-virgin olive oil
- 2 tablespoons fresh lemon juice
- 1 teaspoon dried oregano
- 1 teaspoon dried basil
- 1 teaspoon dried thyme
- 1 teaspoon dried rosemary
- 2 cloves garlic, minced
- Salt and black pepper, to taste

For the Grilled Mahi-Mahi:

- 4 mahi-mahi fillets (about 6-8 ounces each)
- Olive oil for brushing
- Lemon wedges, for serving
- Fresh parsley, chopped, for garnish

Instructions:

For the Italian Herb Marinade:

In a bowl, whisk together extra-virgin olive oil, fresh lemon juice, dried oregano, dried basil, dried thyme, dried rosemary, minced garlic, salt, and black pepper to create the Italian herb marinade.

For the Grilled Mahi-Mahi:

Pat the mahi-mahi fillets dry with paper towels.
Brush both sides of each fillet with olive oil to prevent sticking.
Place the mahi-mahi fillets in a shallow dish and brush them with the Italian herb marinade, ensuring they are well-coated. Marinate for at least 15-30 minutes.
Preheat your grill to medium-high heat.
Grease the grill grates with a bit of oil to prevent sticking.
Place the marinated mahi-mahi fillets on the preheated grill and cook for about 3-4 minutes per side, or until the fish is cooked through and has a nice grill mark.

While grilling, you can brush the fillets with any remaining Italian herb marinade for added flavor.
Once done, transfer the grilled mahi-mahi to a serving platter.
Serve the Italian Herb Grilled Mahi-Mahi hot, garnished with fresh chopped parsley and accompanied by lemon wedges on the side.
Enjoy this Italian-inspired dish with a side of roasted vegetables, risotto, or a light salad for a delicious and herby meal.